Andersonville Prison: The History of the Civil War's Most Notorious Prison Camp

By Charles River Editors

John L. Ransom's aerial depiction of Andersonville

About Charles River Editors

Charles River Editors provides superior editing and original writing services across the digital publishing industry, with the expertise to create digital content for publishers across a vast range of subject matter. In addition to providing original digital content for third party publishers, we also republish civilization's greatest literary works, bringing them to new generations of readers via ebooks.

Sign up here to receive updates about free books as we publish them, and visit Our Kindle Author Page to browse today's free promotions and our most recently published Kindle titles.

Introduction

Andersonville

"Wuld that I was an artist & had the material to paint this camp & all its horors or the tounge of some eloquent Statesman and had the privleage of expresing my mind to our hon. rulers at Washington, I should gloery to describe this hell on earth where it takes 7 of its ocupiants to make a shadow." - Sgt. David Kennedy

"There is so much filth about the camp that it is terrible trying to live here." - Michigan cavalryman John Ransom

Notorious, a hell on earth, a cesspool, a death camp, and infamous have all been used by prisoners and critics to describe Andersonville Prison, constructed to house Union prisoners of war in 1864, and all descriptions apply. Located in Andersonville, Georgia and known colloquially as Camp Sumter, Andersonville only served as a prison camp for 14 months, but during that time 45,000 Union soldiers suffered there, and nearly 13,000 died. Victims found at the end of the war who had been held at Camp Sumter resembled victims of Auschwitz, starving and left to die with no regard for human life.

Rumors about the horrors of Andersonville were making the rounds by the summer of 1864, and they were bad enough that during the Atlanta campaign, Union General William Tecumseh Sherman gave orders for a cavalry raid attempting to liberate the prisoners there. The Union cavalry were repulsed by Southern militia and cavalry at that point, and even after Sherman took Atlanta, the retreating Confederates moved under the assumption that the Union would target Andersonville yet again.

Before the end of the war, the Confederates were moving prisoners from Andersonville to Camp Lawton, but by then, Andersonville was already synonymous with horror. Unable to supply its own armies, the Confederates had inadequately supplied the prison and its thousands of Union prisoners, leaving over 25% of the prisoners to die of starvation and disease. All told, Andersonville accounted for 40% of the deaths of all Union prisoners in the South, and the causes of death included malnutrition, disease, poor sanitation, overcrowding, and exposure to inclement weather.

In fact, Andersonville infuriated the North so much that Henry Wirz, the man in charge of Andersonville, was the only Confederate executed after the war. Before the war, Wirz was a Swiss doctor who had practiced medicine in Kentucky, but while some Southern scholars continue to believe he was simply a victim of circumstance, plenty of evidence suggests his actions were far more insidious and deadly. As the debate over Wirz's fate suggests, one lingering argument in the analysis of Andersonville is whether the abuse and starvation of prisoners was a tragic circumstance of wartime conditions and poverty in the South or if the mistreatment was purposeful and intended. Most scholarship supports the latter point of view, and for the most part, the major dissenting views come from Southern writers and historians who espouse the "Lost Cause." There were articles of war and specific rules on how to treat prisoners on both sides, but by any measurement, humane treatment was all but nonexistent at Andersonville.

Andersonville Prison: The History of the Civil War's Most Notorious Prison Camp chronicles the history of the Civil War's most infamous prison. Along with pictures of important people, places, and events, you will learn about Andersonville like never before, in no time at all.

Andersonville Prison: The History of the Civil War's Most Notorious Prison Camp
About Charles River Editors
Introduction
   Chapter 1: 1864 and the Breakdown of Prisoner Exchanges
   Chapter 2: The Layout of Andersonville
   Chapter 3: Food and Water
   Chapter 4: Daily Life in Andersonville:
   Chapter 5: Escaping Andersonville
   Chapter 6: The End of the Misery
   Chapter 7: Henry Wirz
   Chapter 8: The Legacy of Andersonville
   Additional Online Resources
   Bibliography

Chapter 1: 1864 and the Breakdown of Prisoner Exchanges

Failing to secure the capture of any major northern cities, or the recognition of Great Britain or France, or the complete destruction of any northern armies, the Confederacy's last chance to survive the Civil War was the election of 1864. Democrats had been pushing an anti-war stance or at least a stance calling for a negotiated peace for years, so the South hoped that if a Democrat defeated President Lincoln, or if anti-war Democrats could retake the Congress, the North might negotiate peace with the South. In the election of 1862, anti-war Democrats made some gains in Congress and won the governorship of the State of New York. Confederates were therefore hopeful that trend would continue to the election of 1864.

Lincoln's appreciation for aggressive fighters had made him a defender of Ulysses S. Grant as far back as 1862. In April 1862, Grant's army had won the biggest battle in the history of North America to date at Shiloh, with nearly 24,000 combined casualties among the Union and Confederate forces. Usually the winner of a major battle is hailed as a hero, but Grant was hardly a winner at Shiloh. The Battle of Shiloh took place before costlier battles at places like Antietam and Gettysburg, so the extent of the casualties at Shiloh shocked the nation. Moreover, at Shiloh the casualties were viewed as needless; Grant was pilloried for allowing the Confederates to take his forces by surprise, as well as the failure to build defensive earthworks and fortifications, which nearly resulted in a rout of his army. Speculation again arose that Grant had a drinking problem, and some even assumed he was drunk during the battle. Though the Union won, it was largely viewed that their success owed to the heroics of General William Tecumseh Sherman in rallying the men and Don Carlos Buell arriving with his army, and General Buell was happy to receive the credit at Grant's expense.

Lincoln's steadfastness ensured that Grant's victories out West continued to pile up, and after Vicksburg and Chattanooga, Grant had effectively ensured Union control of the states of Kentucky and Tennessee, as well as the entire Mississippi River. Thus, at the beginning of 1864, Lincoln put him in charge of all federal armies, a position that required Grant to come east.

Grant had already succeeded in achieving two of President Lincoln's three primary directives for a Union victory: the opening of the Mississippi Valley Basin, and the domination of the corridor from Nashville to Atlanta. If he could now seize Richmond, he would achieve the third.

Before beginning the Overland Campaign against Lee's army, Grant, Sherman and Lincoln devised a new strategy that would eventually implement total war tactics. Grant aimed to use the Army of the Potomac to attack Lee and/or take Richmond. Meanwhile, General Sherman, now in command of the Department of the West, would attempt to take Atlanta and strike through Georgia. In essence, having already cut the Confederacy in half with Vicksburg campaign, he now intended to bisect the eastern half.

On top of all that, Grant and Sherman were now intent on fully depriving the Confederacy of the ability to keep fighting. Sherman put this policy in effect during his March to the Sea by confiscating civilian resources and literally taking the fight to the Southern people. For Grant, it meant a war of attrition that would steadily bleed Lee's Army of Northern Virginia. To take full advantage of the North's manpower, in 1864 the Union also ended prisoner exchanges to ensure that the Confederate armies could not be bolstered by paroled prisoners.

"The Peacemakers," a painting depicting Lincoln, Grant, Sherman, and Admiral Porter

Thus, by 1864, things were looking so bleak for the South that the Confederate war strategy was simply to ensure Lincoln lost reelection that November, with the hope that a new Democratic president would end the war and recognize the South's independence. At the same time, the end of the prisoner exchanges compelled the South to build a large prison camp such as the one at Andersonville.

Even before the policy change, the prisoner exchange, which had flourished during the early years of the war, was complicated. Though it's hard to imagine today, the two sides used a parole system by which prisoners were let go after promising not to rejoin the fighting until they had officially been exchanged. Still, there were problems inherent in the system. For example, the sides had to determine how many privates were equal to an officer; for example, several privates were to be exchanged for one officer, and the higher the officer's rank, the more enlisted men had to be sacrificed.

Moreover, the South did not recognize black Union soldiers as real soldiers but instead saw them as "rebel slaves. It reached the point that the Union threatened to summarily execute Confederate prisoners if black soldiers weren't treated as normal prisoners, and the death knell of the prisoner exchange came in the wake of the Fort Pillow Massacre in April 1864.

Confederate cavalry commander Nathan Bedford Forrest already had a controversial Civil War record entering 1864, but he was about to participate in perhaps the most controversial battle of the war. After functioning as an independent raider for the next several months, on April 12, 1864, units of Forrest's cavalry surrounded Fort Pillow on the Mississippi River, north of Memphis. Ironically, the fort had been built in 1861 and named after General Gideon Pillow, the same General Pillow who proved wildly incompetent at Fort Donelson and ignored Forrest's suggestion to escape the siege instead of surrendering to Grant.

Forrest

As far as skirmishes go, Fort Pillow was a completely unremarkable fight. Before attacking, Forrest demanded the unconditional surrender of the Union garrison, a normal custom of his, and he warned the Union commanding officer that he would not be responsible for his soldiers' actions if the warning went unheeded. What made Fort Pillow markedly different was that a sizable amount of the Union garrison defending the Fort was comprised of black soldiers, which particularly enraged Confederate soldiers whenever they encountered those they viewed as former slaves in the field.

It is still unclear exactly how the fighting unfolded, but what is clear is that an unusually high percentage of Union soldiers were killed, and the Confederates were accused of massacring black soldiers after they had surrendered. Primary sources tell conflicting accounts of what happened at Battle of Fort Pillow, leaving scholars to piece together the battle and determine whether Confederate soldiers purposely shot Union soldiers after they had surrendered..

News of the "Fort Pillow Massacre" quickly spread across the country, and it enraged the North. Black soldiers across the country began wearing patches that simply read, "Remember Fort Pillow", and the outrage was instrumental in forcing the Union to threaten to execute Confederate prisoners of war if the Union's black soldiers were not treated properly when captured themselves. Arguments over whether a massacre actually occurred, and what role Forrest played in it, continue to this day. Recent Forrest biographer Brian Steel Wills, taking his subject's past into account, labeled evidence of Forrest's participation in a massacre at Fort Pillow "circumstantial or questionable," claiming Forrest's war record "does not substantiate this charge." Fort Pillow historian Richard Fuchs charges Forrest with full complicity in the massacre, arguing that pro-Forrest arguments appear "designed to prevent any distraction from the hero worship" of Forrest. Author Shelby Foote credited Forrest for "doing all he could to end" the slaughter, while author Robert Browning Jr. argued that since Forrest "lost control of his men," he "shoulders the responsibility for the unnecessary deaths."

While General Forrest conceded that unarmed black soldiers were indeed killed, he would not specify whether this had taken place during or after the battle, either upon his orders or from one of his field commanders. All Forrest confirmed in his report was that "the river was dyed with blood of the slaughtered troops for two hundred yards." Forrest also noted in the report, "The approximate loss was upward of five hundred killed, but few of the officers escaping. My loss was about twenty killed. It is hoped that these facts will demonstrate to the Northern people that negro soldiers cannot cope with Southerners."

By May 1864, the Fort Pillow affair became a matter of Congressional investigations, with many leaders from both Union and Confederate camps anxious to condemn Forrest simply on principle alone. Certainly those who had personally experienced his temper and knew of his volatile reputation could easily imagine him capable of a massacre. Somewhat surprisingly, one of the men who believed Forrest was not guilty of an intentional massacre was General Sherman, who by 1864 begrudgingly admired his troublesome adversary. Based on statements taken from many of his own men who had been taken prisoner by Forrest and attested that "he was usually very kind to them," Sherman stated, "No doubt Forrest's men acted like a set of barbarians, shooting down the helpless negro garrison after the fort was in their possession; but I am told that Forrest personally disclaims any active participation in the assault. I also take it for granted that Forrest did not lead the assault in person, and consequently that he was to the rear, out of sight if not of hearing at the time."

Regardless, Fort Pillow permanently marred Forrest's reputation for the rest of his life, and it was featured prominently in his obituaries throughout the North in 1877. It was also responsible for the primary breakdown of the exchanges, and with that, prisons on both sides were allowed to profligate and grow. This was especially true of Camp Sumter in Georgia. As the leaders of the Confederacy realized that it needed additional fortification to imprison Union soldiers, they decided upon Andersonville, Georgia because of its location: "In late 1863, the Confederacy found that it needed to construct additional prisoner of war camps to house captured Union soldiers waiting to be exchanged. As leaders discussed where to place these new camps, former Georgia governor, Major General Howell Cobb stepped forward to suggest the interior of his home state. Citing southern Georgia's distance from the front lines, relative immunity to Union cavalry raids, and easy access to railroads, Cobb was able to convince his superiors to build a camp in Sumter County. In November 1863, Captain W. Sidney Winder was dispatched to find a suitable location. Arriving at the tiny village of Andersonville, Winder found what he believed to be an ideal site. Located near the Southwestern [1]Railroad, Andersonville possessed transit access and a good water source. With the location secured, Captain Richard B. Winder was sent to Andersonville to design and oversee the construction of the prison. Planning a facility for 10,000 prisoners, Winder designed a 16.5 acre rectangular compound that had a stream flowing through the center. Naming the prison Camp Sumter in January 1864, Winder used local slaves to construct the compound's walls."[2]

---

1 Andersonville Prison Camp. Retrieved at http://www.history.net.com/andersonville-prison-camp
2. American Civil War: Andersonville Prison. Retrieved at http://militaryhistory.about.com./od/civil war/p/andersonville.htm

Chapter 2: The Layout of Andersonville

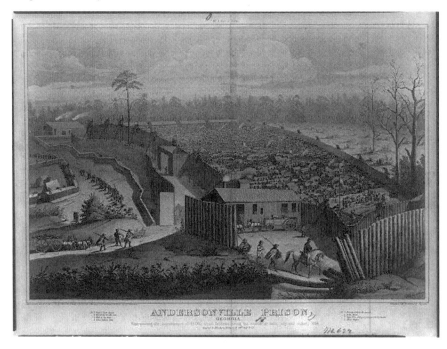

A depiction of Andersonville

As the issue of prisoners became worse, the South decided to erect a prison camp at Andersonville, about 100 miles south of Atlanta. The prison was built on 10.6 acres and was approximately 1,000 feet wide and nearly 780 feet wide. The walls of the stockade were built from pine logs set in a trench five feet deep, and prisoners later complained that the walls of the stockade were so close together that nothing could be seen on the outside. There was also a short fence built in front of the stockade called a "deadline" to keep prisoners away from the stockade walls: "The prison pen was surrounded by a stockade of hewed pine logs that varied in height from 15 to 17 feet. Sentry boxes—called "pigeon roosts" by the prisoners—stood at 90-foot intervals along the top of the stockade and there were two entrances on the west side. Inside, about 19 feet from the wall, was the "deadline," which prisoners were forbidden to cross. The "deadline" was intended to prevent prisoners from climbing over the stockade or from tunneling under it. It was marked by a simple post and rail fence and guards had orders to shoot any prisoner who crossed the fence, or even reached over it. A branch of Sweetwater Creek, called Stockade Branch, flowed through the prison yard and was the only source of water for most of the prison."

John McElroy, a prisoner at Andersonville who went on to write one of the most famous accounts of the camp, wrote of the layout, "The pen was longest due north and south. It was divided in the center by a creek about a yard wide and ten inches deep, running from west to east. On each side of this was a quaking bog of slimy ooze one hundred and fifty feet wide, and so yielding that one attempting to walk upon it would sink to the waist. From this swamp the sand-hills sloped north and south to the stockade. All the trees inside the stockade, save two, had been cut down and used in its construction. All the rank vegetation of the swamp had also been cut off."

In fact, McElroy and some prisoners with him reached Andersonville before the stockade itself was completed. At the time, the Southerners were using slaves to finish off the wall: "The stockade was not quite finished at the time of our arrival—a gap of several hundred feet appearing at the southwest corner. A gang of about two hundred negros were at work felling trees, hewing legs, and placing them upright in the trenches. We had an opportunity—soon to disappear forever—of studying the workings of the "peculiar institution" in its very home. The negros were of the lowest field-hand class, strong, dull, ox-like, but each having in our eyes an admixture of cunning and secretiveness that their masters pretended was not in them. Their demeanor toward us illustrated this. We were the objects of the most supreme interest to them, but when near us and in the presence of a white Rebel, this interest took the shape of stupid, open-eyed, open-mouthed wonder, something akin to the look on the face of the rustic lout, gazing for the first time upon a locomotive or a steam threshing machine. But if chance threw one of them near us when he thought himself unobserved by the Rebels, the blank, vacant face lighted up with an entirely different expression. He was no longer the credulous yokel who believed the Yankees were only slightly modified devils, ready at any instant to return to their original horn-and-tail condition and snatch him away to the bluest kind of perdition; he knew, apparently quite as well as his master, that they were in some way his friends and allies, and he lost no opportunity in communicating his appreciation of that fact, and of offering his services in any possible way. And these offers were sincere."

Once the camp was completed, Clark Thorp described the dimensions of Andersonville this way: "At the time we arrived [in early May 1864] I suppose there were about 15 to 18 acres enclosed by a huge fence, built by hewing pine logs, 24 feet long, on two sides and placing them tight in the ground, about eight feet deep, leaving 16 feet out of the ground. At a distance of about two hundred feet apart, outside the stockade, there were rude ladders erected leading to a platform about twelve or thirteen feet above the ground, on which the guards stood. They were protected from the sun's rays and from storms by a rough board roof…The height of the platform would give the guard easy oversight of the interior of the prison and the top of the stockade made a good rest for his gun. Many of the guards lost no opportunity to shoot at a Yank. There was a dead-line, formed by driving stakes into the ground, leaving about three feet high and sixteen feet from the Stockade. On these stakes were placed sticks of wood 1" x 3." Beyond this line none dared to go unless he wished to commit suicide."

Jud McCranie's picture of the stockade replica erected at Andersonville National Historical Site

As Thorp's account suggests, the dead-line, a short fence a few feet from the stockade, was zealously guarded to prevent the prisoners from scaling the walls and escaping, which was an almost impossible task to begin with. John Maile explained the dead-line as follows: "The 'dead line' formed a complete circuit parallel to the inside of the stockade and about twenty feet therefrom. It consisted of a narrow strip of [22]board nailed to a row of stakes, which were about four feet high. Shoot any prisoner who touches the 'dead line' was the standing order to the guards. Several companies from Georgia regiments were detailed for the duty, and their muskets were loaded with 'buck and ball' (*i. e.*, a large bullet and two buckshot). The day guard at the stockade consisted of one hundred and eighty-six men; the day reserve of eighty-six men. The night reserve consisted of one hundred and ten men; the outlay pickets of thirty-eight men.[25]

Many prisoners were very frightened of the dead-line and recounted tales of accidental crossings, but some crossed it intentionally in an effort to induce the guards to shoot them and

---

25. Prison Life in Andersonville, by John Maile

thus let them escape the hell of Andersonville in death. Martin E. Hogan reflected on the deadline and how an occasional prisoner would cross the dead-line on purpose: "That dead-line was a slight wooden railing [some three feet] it was on a little upright posts, running inside of the stockade...The horrors of that prison were so great that one man went over the line, and refused to leave it until he was hot dead. So great was the horror and misery of that place that I myself had thoughts of going over that dead-line to be shot in preference to living there.

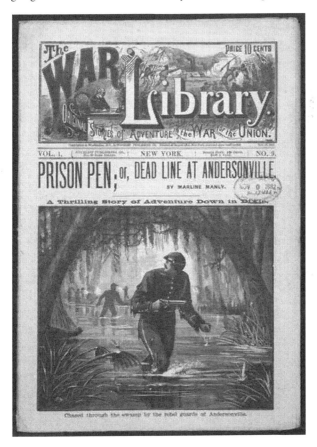

An 1882 story featuring the dead-line

As fate would have it, prisoners arrived before the proposed barracks could ever be built, so the only buildings included a commissary and a hospital surrounded by a stockade and various sentry posts for guards. Since the camp was an open-air cesspool where men could not take shelter against the elements of weather, prisoners were forced to use tents made of blankets or cardboard or fashion a shelter in the dirt underground. The lack of shelter was vividly described by one writer: "Here was a picture of squalor and misery seldom equaled in the sight of man— thousands of men, many of them nearly naked, barefoot, black and filthy beyond the power of words to describe. The space inside was covered, in great part, by rude shelters of all descriptions and sizes, from the some-what commodious tent made by sewing two army blankets together and stretching them over a ridge-pole and pinning the outer ends to the ground, under which several men could crawl for shelter, to a little affair, made by stretching shirts, blouses, etc., in like manner, which could scarcely shelter two men."[5]

    The lack of shelter at Andersonville were also described by Thorp: "We had now been in captivity about eight months and our clothing was in rags though we had been careful to keep it. You must understand that the Confederate government made no attempt to house its Andersonville prisoners….Here we were, by the thousands, taking the weather night and day as it came, without any covering except the clothes worn throughout the twenty-four hours. Let me say here that during June and July 1864 it rained for twenty-one consecutive days and the rainfall amounted at times almost to a deluge. During a heavy storm none of us could keep from getting soaked [2]and those poor fellows who were without any shelter were much worse off than those who had only a blanket for a roof…Many of the men had no clothing or blankets to protect themselves, and at night, would dig into the banks and crawl in until they were nearly hidden and often, when a heavy rain came up, the earth would become loosened and cave in, burying all the men sleeping in the hole or cave. I have seen several pairs of feet projecting out of the ground in the morning after a rain."[6]

    McElroy also wrote about how heavy it rained during his early days at Andersonville: "About the middle of March the windows of heaven opened, and it began a rain like that of the time of Noah. It was tropical in quantity and persistency, and arctic in temperature. For dreary hours that lengthened into weary days and nights, and these again into never-ending weeks, the driving, drenching flood poured down upon the sodden earth, searching the very marrow of the five thousand hapless men against whose chilled frames it beat with pitiless monotony, and soaked the sand bank upon which we lay until it was like a sponge filled with ice-water. It seems to me now that it must have been two or three weeks that the sun was wholly hidden behind the dripping clouds, not shining out once in all that time. The intervals when it did not rain were rare and short. An hour's respite would be followed by a day of steady, regular pelting of the great rain drops. I find that the report of the Smithsonian Institute gives the average annual rainfall in the section around Andersonville, at fifty-six inches —nearly five feet—while that of foggy England is only thirty-two. Our experience would lead me to think that we got the five feet all at once."

---

5. The Sights Fairly Sicken Me, Ural, Susannah J., Civil War Times. Oct2014, Vol. 53 Issue 5, p56-63.
6. Inside Andersonville, by Clark N. Thorp

In addition to the elements, Thorp wrote vividly of the overcrowding:

> "There were no regular streets except the two running into the stockade from the two gates. Spaces were reserved at intervals where men could get into line to be counted. All other spaces were filled up as any man, or squad, chose in pitching their tents....I speak of tents, not because we all had them by any means, but because many were fortunate enough to have one or a portion of one and if so it meant a great deal—it became a question of life or death to us.
>
> I have seen men, by the hundred, standing huddled together for mutual warmth and support (you could not fall very well with men on every side standing tight to you) but these men were weakened by disease and starvation, and during the night many would have to lie down and, in the morning, if it had rained hard you would approach a man who looked like a pile of sand, the heavy rain having thrown sand over his prostrate body. Many of them would be dead in the morning and would be carried out to the deadhouse by their comrades."[7]

One account on May 2, 1864 from Robert H. Kellogg, a sergeant major in the 16th Regiment Connecticut volunteers, recalled the following conditions present upon entering the prison: "As we entered the place, a spectacle met our eyes that almost froze our blood with horror, and made our hearts fail within us. Before us were forms that had once been active and erect;—*stalwart men*, now nothing but mere walking skeletons, covered with filth and vermin. Many of our men, in the heat and intensity of their feeling, exclaimed with earnestness. 'Can this be hell?' 'God protect us!' and all thought that He alone could bring them out alive from so terrible a place. In the center of the whole was a swamp, occupying about three or four acres of the narrowed limits, and a part of this marshy place had been used by the prisoners as a sink, and excrement covered the ground, the scent arising from which was suffocating. The ground allotted to our ninety was near the edge of this plague-spot, and how we were to live through the warm summer weather in the midst of such fearful surroundings, was more than we cared to think of just then."[8]

Chapter 3: Food and Water

A picture of prisoners cramped in Andersonville

"The supreme indifference with which the Rebels always treated the matter of cooking utensils for us, excited my wonder. It never seemed to occur to them that we could have any more need of vessels for our food than cattle or swine. Never, during my whole prison life, did I see so much as a tin cup or a bucket issued to a prisoner. Starving men were driven to all sorts of shifts for want of these. Pantaloons or coats were pulled off and their sleeves or legs used to draw a mess's meal in. Boots were common vessels for carrying water, and when the feet of these gave way the legs were ingeniously closed up with pine pegs, so as to form rude leathern buckets. Men whose pocket knives had escaped the search at the gates made very ingenious little tubs and buckets, and these devices enabled us to get along after a fashion." – John McElroy

A creek ran through the middle of the prison, and while it was supposed to deliver potable water in theory, overcrowding turned that water into a latrine. Furthermore, even aside from the overcrowding, efforts were made to make sure the prisoners did not have clean water; the only place in the creek to get clean water was in the middle of the creek away from the sludge and waste, yet Wirz and his men put ropes up along the edge of the creek to prevent prisoners from getting the clean water in the middle. In addition, Wirz and his cohorts lived upstream and had the cleanest water. Upstream the cooks dumped refuse and grease into the water. Put simply, "Sanitation was lax and feces and other waste products dumped upstream often traveled to soldiers drinking the water lower down." [9]

Wirz

Thorp wrote movingly about the small stream of water all the prisoners had to live on and the punishment they suffered when trying to obtain clean water near the dead-line: "A sluggish stream separated the north from the south side of the prison and this was all the provision made by the Johnnies for the drink needed by the prisoners. This stream was surrounded by wet, marshy ground which was unfit for men to camp in, nor could they occupy all of the hill-side so that much of the space was worthless as a camp, but very valuable as a source of disease and death. The water would spread out over this low ground, especially near the west or upper side of the stockade. Into this the men would wade by the hundreds, with the canteens of their squads upon their backs, waiting their turn to get near the dead-line, where they might reach above the muddy water, to get some which was clear. [If the] wrong kind of a guard happened to be on duty, he was apt to get a bullet into his head."

Another description of the scant water supply was sobering: "The only water supply was a stream that first trickled through a Confederate army camp, then pooled to form a swamp inside the stockade. It provided the only source of water for drinking, bathing, cooking, and sewage. Under such unsanitary conditions, it wasn't surprising when soldiers began dying in staggering numbers."

John Maile, a Union prisoner, wrote about how the water flowed and what forces of nature and man made it so putrid: "The surface of the interior consisted of two hillsides, sloping respectively north and south towards the center which was occupied by a swamp of nearly four acres. This was traversed by a sluggish creek which was some five feet wide and six inches deep, and made its way along the foot of the south slope. Up the stream were located the headquarters of Capt. Wirz, the [3]camps of the Confederate artillery and infantry and the cook-house for the prisoners. The drainage of these localities entered the creek which flowed into the prison through spaces between the stockade timbers, and polluted the water which was the chief supply of the prison, and which, at midnight, in its clearest condition, was the color of amber. The intervening space at the foot of the north hill was a wide morass, and when overflowed by rains became a vast cesspool on which boundless swarms of flies settled down and laid their eggs; which were speedily hatched by the fervent heat of the nearly tropical sun, and became a horrible undulating mass. On a change of wind the odor could be detected miles away; indeed it was reported that the people of Macon petitioned General Howell Cobb, the military governor of Georgia, for a removal of the prison located sixty miles away, lest an awful pestilence sweep over their country!"[11]

Throughout the camp, many prisoners started to dig wells in hopes of getting access to clean water, and while they had a hard time fashioning equipment for such a task, but many prisoners managed. Thorp explained, "During June it became quite the fashion to dig wells. Many wells were dug and the condition of a large part of the prisoners was much improved. The party with whom I associated were fortunate enough to secure good water at [4]a distance of about 18 feet down. The soil was sandy and apt to cave so that it was necessary to dig the well considerable wider at the top so that it would have quite a slope to prevent caving in. The means used for removing the earth were generally a pair of pants legs tied at the bottom and were hauled up with ropes made from strips of clothing, blankets, etc."[12]

John Maile noted that some Confederates helped dig wells for fresh water, even though many of men tried to dig tunnels to escape. If the prisoners were only interested in water and not

---

9. Inside Andersonville, by Clark Thorp
10. Andersonville Prison. Retrieved at http://www.newworldencyclopedia.org/entry/Andersonville_prison

11. The Project Gutenberg EBook of Prison Life in Andersonville, by John L. Maile. Retrieved at http://www.gutenberg.org/files/39584/39584-h/39584-h.htm
12. Inside Andersonville, by Clark Thorp
13. Prison Life in Andersonville by John L. Maile

attempting escape, occasional permission was granted to keep the wells open: "As the killed and wounded are scattered over the fields of the sanguinary battle, so our dying sick lay around on every hand. In the early summer, Capt. Wirz issued to the prisoners picks and shovels, with which to dig wells for increased water supply. From some of these wells the men started tunnels through which to escape. Discovering this, the commander withdrew the tools, and ordered the wells to be filled up. Permission to keep one of them open was purchased by a group of prisoners. It was sunk to a necessary depth, covered with a platform and trap door, and supplied about one thousand men."[13]

Not surprisingly, the rations provided at Andersonville were substandard; not only was there not enough food, it was not the right kind of food and it was not well-prepared. First, soldiers had to stand in long lines to organize and be counted for the 4:00 p.m. rations, and if they weren't in line for morning roll call or were too sick to stand in line, they simply didn't receive rations for the day. John Maile explained, "At ten o'clock every forenoon a drum call was beaten from the platform at the south gate. At this signal the prisoners fell into line by detachments, forming as best they could in the narrow paths that separated the small tents, blanket shanties or dug-outs. At the same moment a company of Confederate [5]sergeants entered the two gates for the purpose of counting and recording the number of the prisoners. To each of these officers a certain number of detachments were assigned. The men, unsheltered from the fierce sun-heat, had perforce to remain standing during the entire count. If a number less than that of yesterday was in evidence, the Federal sergeant had to account for the deficit. Sometimes a number of men were too ill to stand up, so the line was held the longer while the Confederate official viewed the sick where they lay."[14]

When 4:00 came around, the men fought for every crumb:

"At four o'clock in the afternoon rations of corn bread and bacon were issued on the basis of the morning count of those who are able to stand up. Two army wagons drawn by mules entered the north and south gates simultaneously. They were piled high with bread, thin loaves of corn bread or Johnny cake, made of coarse meal and water by our men who had been paroled for that work.

A blanket was spread upon the ground and the quantity for a detachment was placed thereon in three piles; one for every ninety, according to the number of men able to eat. In like manner the sergeants of nineties sub-divided the piles to the thirties.

The writer had charge of a division of thirty and distributed as follows: His blanket was spread in front of his shelter tent and on it he spread the bread in as many pieces as there were men counted in the morning.

---
[14] Prison Life in Andersonville, by John L. Maile.

Each man had his number and was intently watching the comparative size of the portions. 'Sergeant,' cries one, pointing to a cube of bread, 'That piece is smaller than the one next to it.' A crumb is taken from the one and place upon the other. The relative size of any piece may be challenged by any member of the thirty, for his life is involved."[15]

Prisoners dropped like flies from malnutrition and scurvy because, as Thorp noted, daily rations consisted a small piece of cornbread and uncooked bacon in very small amounts, with occasional beans, cowpeas, or rice: "The diet consisted of cornbread, raw bacon at times and cowpeas at times. Our provisions were very much short of the necessary. If cooked rations were issued we would get a piece of corn-bread about 2" x 2" x 3," the meal being ground cob and all, coarser than one in the north would buy for his horse, a few beans (perhaps one-half pint) and a couple of ounces of pork or bacon…. Soon the meat supply failed and I have seen a team loaded up high with the under jaws of hogs, smoked and old, and as we did not get a jaw-bone to each man you may guess that we were not fattened by them."[16]

Another soldier, John H. Goldsmith of the 14th regiment Illinois infantry, had this to say about the food: "I had charge of the rations up to the time I left the prison. The rations consisted of half a pound of meal of very poor quality, half a pound of beef, half a pound of peas and two gills of molasses. The ration of molasses was on each alternate day, and of beef the same day…The rations issued to our [6]prisoners was just one-half the quantity issued to the rebel troops."[17]

One prisoner, George A. Hitchcock, wrote about the horrors of scurvy as he began suffering from it in September 1864: "Signs of scurvy have appeared in my mouth around the gums of my diseased teeth. The gums swell up and turn dark purple. Where others have it and do not recover, this swelling spreads in a few days until the face and neck turn black as if blood settled all over it; then the teeth drop out -- the jaws become set and a general rotting process is the last stage. With others the disease shows itself first in the limbs, rendering them stiff and helpless. My general feeling is one of complete lassitude and low spirits."[18]

Thorp also had much to say about the horrors of scurvy due to a diet totally lacking in Vitamin C: "Privations, lack of vegetable food and lack of exercise [led many of us to contract that] dread disease, scurvy. The mouth would become infected, the gums swollen so the teeth could not be closed together and we would be unable to chew any solid food. The gums would

15. Prison Life in Andersonville, by John L. Maile

16. Inside Andersonville, by Clark N. Thorp

17. The Tragedy of Andersonville: Trial of Captain Henry Wirz, the Prison Keeper By Norton Parker Chipman

18. The Sights Fairly Sicken me, By Susannah Ural

become black and decayed and, in my own case, with long and sharp fingernails I could gouge away parts, which were in such condition as to be exceedingly offensive to the smell. Limbs would be drawn up to the body and the back of them would become discolored and from the heels to the hips resembled, in color, a very severe black and blue spot. A dropsical swelling of the flesh would take place and I could pull the flesh of my feet out of shape or press an indentation into the flesh and it would remain in that shape until action replaced it."[19]

    Despite how meager the rations were, prisoners quickly learned that it was best to not eat it all at once. According to Maile, "The cube of bread and morsel of meat constitute the ration for twenty-four hours. One-half may be eaten at once; the remainder should be put in the haversack for breakfast. If any one yields to his insatiable hunger and eats the whole for supper he has to fast until the following evening and must then deny himself and put away the portion for the next morning's breakfast."[21]

    Since disease was rampant, many men found themselves in the crudely built hospital, and instead of having white hospital beds and caring nurses, the sick simply suffered more misery. One prisoner, Joseph Adler, recalled, "I should judge the sick were treated badly, the majority of the sick men had to lie on the bare ground; the majority of them had no blankets; they had nothing to lie on and nothing to cover themselves with, and most of the time the food furnished them was unfit for them to eat. A little corn bread and rice soup that I would not give to a dog."[20]

---

19. Inside Andersonville, by Clark Thorp
20. The Tragedy of Andersonville by Chipman

INTERIOR VIEW OF THE HOSPITAL

A sketch depicting the prisoners on the floor of the hospital

Chapter 4: Daily Life in Andersonville:

A picture of prisoners at Andersonville

"The emptying of the prisons at Danville and Richmond into Andersonville went on slowly during the month of March. They came in by train loads of from five hundred to eight hundred, at intervals of two or three days. By the end of the month there were about five thousand in the stockade. There was a fair amount of space for this number, and as yet we suffered no inconvenience from our crowding, though most persons would fancy that thirteen acres of ground was a rather limited area for five thousand men to live, move and have their being a upon. Yet a few weeks later we were to see seven times that many packed into that space." – John McElroy

Many Union soldiers had money, and since 45,000 prisoners moved through Andersonville in the span of about 14 months, there was actually a free market among the prisoners. Since rations, clothing, and shelter were substandard, many shopkeepers and merchants set up shop inside the stockade and sold fresh vegetables of every kind. Thorp recounted this market: "The authorities at Andersonville allowed supplies to be sold to the prisoners for Federal money. Numerous small restaurants flourished in the stockade. From small clay ovens they supplied fresh bread and baked meats. Irish and sweet potatoes, string beans, peas, tomatoes, melons, sweet corn, and other garden products were abundantly offered for sale. New arrivals were amazed to find these resources in the midst of utter destitution and starvation."[23]

In addition to food for the starving men, other services included doctoring, tailoring, and cobbling for worn out shoes. In fact, these kinds of activities led to Andersonville being referred to as one of the largest cities in the Confederacy: "Like most cities (Andersonville was the fifth largest 'city' in the Confederacy), it included a host of tradesmen and merchants. There were [21]representatives of many occupations. Barbers and laundries flourished. There were dentists, doctors, watchmakers, bakers, tailors, and many a cobbler repairing rotting shoes. Prisoners who had money could buy almost anything imaginable to eat. James Selman's shanty periodically offered cucumbers, watermelons, muskmelons, onions, and potatoes. Selman's prices were high because he paid enormous premiums to the farmers and women who brought their produce and baked goods to the camp. (He still made a profit). Selmans' sutlery, was only the most obvious of several grocery alternatives. Over 200 small businesses operated on Market Street inside of the stockade. Full time vendors cried out 'who wants wood?' and 'Here goes a bully dress coat, only $4.'"[21]

Besides an inadequate diet, the men had no clothes to wear except what they had arrived with, so prisoners were inevitably soaked in the Georgia rains and freezing in the cold of the winter. The prisoners wore tatters, and since the water was putrid, they could not wash the clothes they did have. As a result, unless prisoners could afford to buy new clothes from one of markets inside the stockade, they were left to withstand the often cruel elements of weather. Thorp noted:

> "We had now been in captivity about eight months and our clothing was in rags though we had been careful to keep it. You must understand that the Confederate government made no attempt to house its Andersonville prisoners....Here we were, by the thousands, taking the weather night and day as it came, without any covering except the clothes worn throughout the twenty-four hours. Let me say here that during June and July 1864 it rained for twenty-one consecutive days and the rain-fall amounted at times almost to a deluge. During a heavy storm none of us could keep from getting soaked and those poor fellows who were without any shelter were much worse off than those who had only a blanket for a roof.
>
> Many of the men had no clothing or blankets to protect themselves, and at night, would dig into the banks and crawl in until they were nearly hidden [21]and

---

[21] Andersonville, What really happened. http://ecedweb.unomaha.edu/lessons/andersonvilleact4.htm

often, when a heavy rain came up, the earth would become loosened and cave in, burying all the men sleeping in the hole or cave. I have seen several pairs of feet projecting out of the ground in the morning after a rain. Tunneling under the stockade, for the purpose of escape was often undertaken but seldom amounted to anything except hard work and the discouragement of defeat, as in almost all cases some one would inform on them and the Rebels would come in, dig down to the tunnel and fill it up."[22]

Since there were no rules in the camp except punishment for crossing the deadline or tunneling for escape along with other petty crimes, some prisoners formed bands and became robbers. Many of these bandits had enlisted under illegal names and were not model soldiers to begin with, but regardless of the circumstances, they took to robbing new prisoners and stealing everything they owned. Incoming Union prisoners often had money and possessions, while those who had been there for awhile did not, so they were especially vulnerable at the hands of thieves. Thorp mentioned some of the prison slang associated with them: "We termed our habitations 'shebangs,' a sneak thief a 'flanker,' a robber a 'raider.' There being no law within the stockade, evil men among us took to robbing from their comrades. There was an organization of robbers so bold and daring that they would go in squads through the prison and whatever they saw, in the way of clothing or blankets, they captured. For instance, four men would be lying under a fairly good blanket, a raider would come along and lay hold of the blanket and if the men under it attempted to reclaim it each man would quickly receive a blow on the head from a short club in the hands of the raiders companions. [These] raiders committed several cruel and vicious murders. At last the Rebels were appealed to and a guard of a few men under a non-commissioned officer entered the prison and appealed to the Yanks to organize and hunt these desperadoes down."[26]

Some of the Union soldiers fought back by forming their own bands. Known as the "regulators," they countered the "raiders," and the Confederates often helped the regulators against the robbers. In the end, six raiders were actually hanged, and according to Thorp, "All that was necessary to cause swift vengeance to fall upon the heads of the evil-doers was done. They were chased and beaten with clubs and captured. The Confederate authorities rendered assistance in the prosecutions, which followed by allowing a jury to be impaneled and a regular court to be instituted with able lawyers from among the prisoners as judges and counsel for the defense and prosecution. The witnesses were subpoenaed, and after a fair and impartial trial, six of the raiders were convicted and hanged, and from that time forward flanking and raiding were unknown among the prisoners."[27]

Andersonville brought out the worst in people, but some examples of kindness could be found in the camp. Thorp shared an anecdote of how medical stewards helped him when he became too

---

[22] Prison Life in Andersonville, by John L. Maile.

sick to function any longer:

> "In the month of July, I became so helpless that a few friends volunteered to carry me out to the gate, in hopes that I might be admitted to the hospital. Many poor fellows as helpless as myself were borne by comrades and laid upon the ground near the gates, waiting for the hour to come when they could be seen by Doctors, on the outside of the inner gate.
>
> Here we lay in the broiling sun, between two stockades where no breath of air could come and many of us were not even looked at by the doctors. During the day one-horse wagons were used as ambulances in carrying the sick to the hospital....On being taken from the ambulance I was set upon the ground among a lot of other comrades. Soon a hospital steward came along and eight of us were assigned to the first tent in the ward, where we slept protected from the weather for the first time since the 1st day of May. Our rations were not materially different, but we received some medicine for our scurvy, although not very much to brag about. The medicine consisted of less than one pint of, shall I say, swill and prepared thus: a bushel or so of corn-meal was put into a barrel at the head of the ward and filled with water from a neighboring swamp, a stream from which ran across the lower end of the hospital grounds, this, when allowed to sour, became the medicine which was to cure our scurvy.
>
> A few days after we had been thus fortunate in securing a tent on entering the hospital, a few boards were hauled into the hospital and unloaded near our tent. We inquired for what purpose and were informed that all tents were to have bunks put into them. The seven men in the tent with me, all scurvy patients, were quite an intelligent body of men and pretty good talkers and we proceeded at once, with arguments, to persuade the hospital steward to have the boards put into our tent first, which he finally consented to do, and for the first time our beds were raised from the ground. Our improvement after this was quite marked.
>
> On being taken from the ambulance I was set upon the ground among a lot of other comrades. Soon a hospital steward came along and eight of us were assigned to the first tent in the ward, where we slept protected from the weather for the first time since the 1st day of May. Our rations were not materially different, but we received some medicine for our scurvy, although not very much to brag about. The medicine consisted of less than one pint of, shall I say, swill and prepared thus: a bushel or so of corn-meal was put into a barrel at the head of the ward and filled with water from a neighboring swamp, a stream from which ran across the lower end of the hospital grounds, this, when allowed to sour, became the medicine which was to cure our scurvy.

A few days after we had been thus fortunate in securing a tent on entering the hospital, a few boards were hauled into the hospital and unloaded near our tent. We inquired for what purpose and were informed that all tents were to have bunks put into them. The seven men in the tent with me, all scurvy patients, were quite an intelligent body of men and pretty good talkers and we proceeded at once, with arguments, to persuade the hospital steward to have the boards put into our tent first, which he finally consented to do, and for the first time our beds were raised from the ground. Our improvement after this was quite marked."[52]

After Thorp received medicine for his scurvy and a roof over his head for the first time, he feared he would lose what had become true privileges at Andersonville. His troubles were not over, because as he remained there laying on the ground, fleas crawled all over him until he appealed again to the kindness of the medical steward:

"Gradually I became able to walk with my limbs a little straighter until I could stand with my knees at an angle of about 90 degrees, resting my weight upon my toes. At this time came the terrible news that our tent was to be used for gangrene patients and the following day we were separated and I never knew what became of my seven comrades.

I was put into a tent which would hold four men but the only occupant when I entered was a poor, moaning helpless wretch who died the same night. There had been as many as four deaths in one day in some of these tents and I presumed this one was as bad as any. Each of these poor fellows was absolutely helpless and had been so for many weeks and each one contributed to the vermin which formed a large part of the floor of the tent. The rest of the floor was sand about 3 or 4 inches deep…no more awful misery could be suffered than fell to my lot that night.

After enduring all that human nature could I took up my abode in the street, about morning, and was there when the steward came around with his assistants and carried out into the street those who had died during the night, which included my tent mate. The steward inquired what I was doing out there. I told him I had moved and preferred to sleep outside. He informed me that I would have to go back into the tent. I told him I would not and called him to witness and, hobbling back into the tent on my toes, I pulled back my sleeves and scooped up a handful of the tent floor. The fleas were constantly springing from the sand scattering much of it and the vermin crawling out would take more of it. I constantly brushed my wrists to keep them from crawling up on my body.

When the sand became quiet in my hand not much more than half of the amount I had scooped up remained, I threw the rest down and turning fiercely upon the steward demanded if he had the heart to see a man put into such a place as that to sleep and telling him that, under no circumstances except being tied in the tent, would I again attempt to occupy it. A parley ensued when he offered me a nurse's tent, with bunks in it, providing I would take the tent which I had formerly vacated and care for the eight gangrene patients with which it had been filled.

During this conversation I had been standing with bent legs and upon my toes and, casting my eyes downward, I said to him, 'I am a pretty subject to attempt to take care of eight men covered with gangrenous sores.' He urged me to take it as it was the only alternative and I accepted and for three hours I stood upon my toes, attending to my patients. One man, among the eight, had 35 open sores."[53]

By helping others, receiving decent lodgings, and the chance to eat rations, Thorp eventually improved and regained his health:

"The exercise, the imperative necessity for hard work, a good place in which to sleep caused my health and condition to rapidly improve and it was not many weeks before I could walk and touch my heels to the ground, with the limbs nearly straight. My mouth, also, gradually improved until I could chew my rations.

While still an inmate of the hospital in the early part of December 1864, the Confederates [attempted to improve the hospital by building sheds with the assistance of Yankee workmen]. Having been a wood-worker previous to [53]entering the army, I was fortunate enough to be selected as one and, after being paroled, wherein we promised not to attempt to escape, we began our work.

You can scarcely imagine the delight with which we hailed our greater liberty, having no guards over us and allowed to roam at will, outside of working hours."[54]

Chapter 5: Escaping Andersonville

Many prisoners tried to escape from Andersonville, but naturally, most escape attempts were unsuccessful. From the beginning, the tight guard over the dead-line and the lack of tools to build tunnels deterred prisoners, and the camp kept bloodhounds that hunted down escaped prisoners and often tore them apart. The punishment for attempting escape was being bucked and whipped, being put into the stocks without food or drink, or wearing a ball and chain.

Black people around Andersonville occasionally suffered punishment for offering invaluable aid to prisoners: "The aid that African Americans gave to Union soldiers fleeing Andersonville

---

53, 54 Inside Andersonville by George Skotch

had its roots in traditional structures used to maintain slavery. Conscripted enslaved laborers built the prison and local whites feared the Yankee presence would fuel slave revolts. In addition, these black workers prepared the ground for escape tunnels and drove the meal wagons that sometimes provided another means of escape."[55] In at least one case, slaves were able to safely get a prisoner to freedom: "After using a tunnel to escape, William L. Farmer of the 111th Illinois Volunteers hid in the swamps a quarter of a mile from the prison, using the water to shield his scent from the hounds. Enslaved African Americans concealed and fed him until they could arrange his transportation to Union lines near Atlanta."[56]

Thorp also attempted an escape with several of his fellow prisoners, and they were assisted by slaves:

> "During [our Sunday] rambles five of the party, with which I was connected, met a colored man from the banks of the Flint River six miles away from Andersonville and, in conversation with him, conceived an idea of escape by way of the Flint River to the blockading squadron in the Appalachian Bay [Apalachee Bay] in the Gulf of Mexico.
>
> Plans were all laid for an escape and the evening set when he agreed to meet us on a certain road and [in trade for blankets and other provisions] pilot us to the Flint River. After having left camp we failed to meet our colored friend but were never able to tell whether through his fault or ours. We started down the river on foot, knowing full well that, in the morning, the Andersonville pack of hungry blood-hounds would be after us.

After going a few miles, the party found a boat and paddles, but when they tried to maneuver it downstream, they came across rapids and other obstacles. Eventually, the group headed back to land, and they found shelter in a railroad depot. Despite facing bloodhounds and Rebel soldiers, the group persisted, thanks in large measure to the fact they were being fed and assisted by slaves:

> "Many Rebel soldiers were evidently taking a train that stood by the depot [so] we began to get away from that river as fast as possible. Keeping in the woods, [we soon] ran across a party of Negro men and women working in a [56]field. I don't know whether they went without their dinner or not, but it was pork-killing time and they brought us a pork stew with corn pones enough for ten men.
>
> [Later the slaves had told us that] a few miles below the city there was a large spring only a short distance from the river. They also told us that 5,000 Rebels were encamped there. After striking the river we followed the bank until we came to the creek formed by the spring. We could see the bottom plainly and supposed we could wade it. Jones soon had his clothing off and commenced to cross the

---

56 Inside Andersonville by George Skotch

creek. By the time he was six feet from shore he was in water up to his neck and we knew that if we crossed that stream we must swim and two of the party could not do that.

After consultation it was deemed best to try and make a circuit around the Rebel camp. [But after encountering a guard at a Rebel outpost, we returned] to the river where we finally induced our timid (they were only afraid of water) comrades to swim. Now commenced a careful march down the river and before daylight we had put many miles between that Rebel camp and ourselves.

Towards morning a heavy fog settled over the river making it difficult and dangerous to proceed. The country appeared to be open and settled, and we concluded to go on in hopes of reaching a wood. When we were compelled to land we found we were in a large grove of young forest trees without underbrush or means of concealment.

We built up a fire, imprudently, of course, and lay down to sleep. When we woke up we found the day well advanced and that the fog had lifted. After some hours we discovered three boys, two black and one white, approaching the grove seated upon two horses. [When they saw us, they turned their horses and galloped off.] Our situation now was nearly hopeless. We were in Mitchell County, Ga., and on the opposite bank was Baker Co., notorious for its numerous packs of blood-hounds. We argued that if we took the boat and proceeded down stream that the pursuing parties would head us off and if we crossed the river into Baker county they would soon have a pack of trained hounds after us.

An hour or so later our expectations of pursuit were realized. A party of four white men and three negroes, mounted upon dripping horses, approached the grove from down stream and the leader, a white man, of 50 or 60 years, with a gun, asked what we were doing there. They were evidently much excited, more so than we were. Leaning on my left elbow and looking up at him I coolly informed him that we were resting a bit and he informed us that he should have to place us under arrest, as he was a confederate soldier on furlough, and would be held accountable if we escaped. We told him that we expected that and were ready to go with him.

[Taken to the old gentleman's home], we were greeted by his son-in-law, a Rebel Major. He invited us to his plantation, where he gave us a good supper, and said that in the morning he would hitch up and let his boys take us over to Newton [to begin] our return trip, putting the best face upon it we could.

Arriving at Newton we were turned over to a Provost Marshall [who] treated us very kindly, furnished us with all the tobacco we wished, loaded us with eatables and peanuts, and locked us in a room in the court house for the night. Having no chairs, beds or blankets, to make us comfortable, we got somewhat restless in the morning and some one of the party, happened to have a pocket-knife, we took off the catch which held the door and when our jailor came he found his prisoners sitting on the court-house steps enjoying his tobacco.

The day was Sunday and we did not march. The following morning we started on foot for Albany. There we were put on a train for Andersonville.

Happening to be the first to step off the car on our arrival, I found myself in front of Captain [Henry] Wirz. He said, 'What is your name?' I told him, 'Thorp.' 'Oh yes, you are the five fellows what runned away last week.' I told him, 'Yes sir, we are the fellows.' The Captain, one of the most violent tempered men I have ever met, flew into a violent passion and began a tirade of abuse interspersed with many oaths and uncomplimentary names. He ordered us to be taken to the little stockade [where] prisoners were severely punished. But, strange to say, we were never punished for an hour. A day or two later we were turned into the stockade.'[57]

For his part, Maile found escape to be almost impossible: "To increase the difficulty of tunnel escape, slaves and teams were employed to build piles of pitch-pine along the cleared space beyond the outer stockade. At night, when these were lighted, a line of fires was made which illuminated a wide area. From these fires arose columns of dense smoke, which in the sultry air of a midsummer night hung like a pall over the silent city of disease and starvation. Yet the city was not wholly quiet, for undertones of thousands of voices that murmured during the day at night died away into the low moans of the sick and the expiring, or rose into the overtones of the outcry of distressful dreams. In the edge of the gloom beyond the fires, patrols paced to and fro until the dawn. Every evening the watch-call sounded, 'Post number one, nine o'clock and all is well.' This cry was repeated by each sentinel until it had traveled around the stockade back to the place of starting. 'Nine and a half o'clock and all is well,' was next spoken, and likewise repeated. Thus every half hour from dark to daylight the time was called off, and this grim challenge greeted our ears every night until the survivors bade the Confederacy good-bye. Not that our captors benevolently wished to increase the sense of the shortness of the time until our release, but to be assured that the guards were keeping awake."[58]

Chapter 6: The End of the Misery

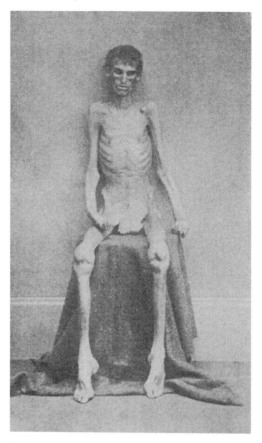

Picture of a surviving prisoner

As the end of the war drew near, Thorp and his fellow captives figured that an exchange of prisoners or outright release was imminent. At this point, it became a battle for survival:

> Spring came at last and rumors of an exchange became more and more frequent, and finally a large number of prisoners were taken from the stockade and sent to Vicksburg. After a few days another party were sent away and you can imagine with what utter despondency those left would see the gates closed and we inside.

At length the day came when we were to leave the stockade, the last of all the thousands who had suffered there. When I glanced around me, on going through the gates, I presume there were not one hundred men following and the stockade was tenantless, forever, thank God.

Thorp and some other prisoners were eventually taken to Jacksonville, where they boarded the USS *Constitution* and were transported to "Camp Parole" in Annapolis. For the first time in months, the Union prisoners received real rations, clothes, and even back pay for their service.[59]

George Hitchcock had this to say about bidding Anderson farewell: "Well, this is about the last of Andersonville for us and it is a general abandoning of this horrid place for orders came for us all to be ready to start at eleven in the forenoon, but as means of transportation did not arrive, we did not start until ten at night when we were roused out of a sound sleep. And went out through the gates in perfect darkness and in a pitting rain, a most fitting [and] appropriate time and aspect for us to pass out of a place that, if we are allowed to live long, will always combine more of the realities which we expect will be found in that dark and terrible region of despair of a future world known as "hell" than any other can to us. Thankful for past favors (we cannot feel too thankful that we have been allowed to remain to see almost the termination of the glorious reign of the Dutch Captain [Wirz]), we cast one (not long lingering) look back into the darkness and pack into old freight cars, eighty three in a car and move out on the northward track toward Macon."[60]

Today, Clara Barton is best known as a nurse who helped soldiers during the Civil War and founded the Red Cross, but she was also primarily responsible for finding all the soldiers who had perished at Andersonville, informing their families of their deaths, and later erecting tombstones for every dead soldier. Dorrence Atwater, who had served in the hospital at Andersonville during his imprisonment, had taken exact notes of every fallen comrade in Andersonville, smuggled his notes through the Confederate guards upon his release, and contacted Clara Barton to obtain her help. "In June of 1865 a young clerk named Dorrence Atwater contacted Barton and requested copies of her lists of missing soldiers. Atwater had been a prisoner at Andersonville and had been paroled to work in the hospital, where he diligently maintained a copy of the death records. Ecstatic, Barton contacted Secretary of War Edwin M. Stanton and asked to accompany the US Army's expedition to Andersonville to identify the graves there. At Andersonville in July and August of 1865, Atwater and Barton poured through the letters she had received, and began to search for these missing soldiers in the Andersonville Death Register and captured hospital records. While laborers worked to erect headboards in the cemetery, Barton wrote dozens of letters informing families that their loved ones had died at Andersonville. At the end of the expedition, Barton was given the honor of raising the American flag for the first time over the recently established Andersonville National Cemetery."[61]

Clara Barton

Andersonville National Cemetery

Barton set up the Missing Soldiers Office and hired clerks, including Atwater, to respond to the numerous letters she had received from families of prisoners at Andersonville. She also helped Atwater when he was court-martialed and ordered to give over his accounts of the dead:

> "After returning from Andersonville, Barton set up the Missing Soldier's Office in Washington in 1865. She hired numerous clerks, including Dorrence Atwater, to respond to the more than 60,000 letters that she received. By the time the Missing Soldiers Office closed in 1867, Barton and her staff had identified more than 20,000 missing soldiers, including nearly 13,000 who had died at Andersonville Prison.

Because of her fame as a nurse, she received much of the credit for the work of the Missing Soldiers Office and the Andersonville expedition. In a post war speaking series she was hailed as the 'Heroine of Andersonville' and toured the nation displaying artifacts that she had collected at the prison site and lectured on the sufferings of the prisoners. She was even inducted as an honorary member of the Andersonville Survivor's Association, and the army's expedition to Andersonville to identify the graves quickly became known as Barton's expedition, even though she had only accompanied the previously planned endeavor and had worked primarily writing letters - not [61]identifying graves as has often been claimed.

Barton's greatest contribution to the Andersonville story is through her work in the Missing Soldiers Office and her support of Dorrence Atwater. Atwater was court-martialed and jailed in the fall of 1865 related to a dispute over the ownership of the Andersonville Death Register. It was through Barton's efforts that he was finally released and she then supported his publication of the Death Register. Barton is often mistakenly given credit for identifying the graves at Andersonville. However, she deserves a great deal of credit for her efforts to account for the missing soldiers, both at Andersonville and across countless battlefields."[61]

Chapter 7: Henry Wirz

Heinrich Hartmann Wirz was born on November 25, 1823, in Zurich, Switzerland, and though he was fated to become notorious across the Atlantic, the details of his various occupations in his early years are sketchy before he moved to the United States in 1849: He had dreams of becoming a doctor, and some accounts have him listed as practicing medicine in both Switzerland and Kentucky before he moved to Louisiana. According to one biographical account:

> "Henry Wirz was born in 1822 in Switzerland. In 1849 he immigrated to the United States and attempted to go into business as a physician in New York City. Failing at this, he moved to Connecticut and then to Northhampton, Massachusetts where he worked as a translator in several small factories. There he took a job working at a water-cure establishment before moving to Kentucky to work as a homeopathic physician. He operated water-cure establishments in Cadiz and Louisville until 1857, when he moved to Louisiana to 'take charge of' Cabin Teele, a 2,200 acre plantation owned by Levin R. Marshall. At Cabin Teele, Wirz continued to practice homeopathic medicine while overseeing the hundreds of slaves in bondage there. This was Wirz's first experience with controlling large numbers of people, a skill that would serve him later.

> At the outset of the Civil War, Wirz enlisted in the 4th Battalion of Louisiana Infantry, organized in his home of Madison, Louisiana. In the aftermath of Bull Run in July 1861, the unit was sent Richmond, where Wirz was assigned to guard duty at Howard's Factory Prison. He immediately began to organize prisoners, and developed a reputation for efficiency and callousness. He was, as one prisoner

---
61 Clara Barton. Columbia Electronic Encyclopedia, 6th Edition. Q1 2014

wrote in 1862, 'the essence of authority at the prison... [he] thought himself omnipresent and omniscient.' By the fall of 1861, Wirz attracted the attention of General John Winder, who at that time was in charge of the Richmond prison system. Winder placed Wirz on detached duty as a part of his prison management team. In November 1861 the Richmond newspapers reported that Sergeant Henry Wirz was one of seven men on the city's Prison Board, charged with ensuring the security of all military prisons in Richmond. Serving with Wirz on this board was Captain George C. Gibbs. Three years later the two men worked together at Andersonville, and Gibbs later testified against his colleague."

After he was injured as a private in the Battle of Seven Pines in 1862, Wirz started working for John H. Winder, who was in charge of Confederate prison camps. One account of Wirz outlined his negative leadership qualities: "As a special assistant to Confederate president Jefferson Davis, Wirz spent a year in Europe acting on behalf of Davis. He returned in 1864 and was selected to oversee the military prison at Andersonville. A difficult and often morose person, Wirz was known to be a weak administrator and to have a bad temper."

Winder

In April 1864, Wirz was put in charge of Andersonville, but while he immediately took control, each set of guards had their own commander, which made the chain of authority difficult to navigate. "Wirz immediately began to reorganize the prison to make it more secure and to improve efficiency. He ordered the construction of a deadline to keep prisoners away from the stockade walls. Drawing on his experience documenting prisoners in 1862, he ordered a daily headcount to be taken. Throughout his time at Andersonville he was frustrated by unclear lines of responsibility. He was charged with daily operations inside the prison – this included taking roll, security, and the issuing of rations and supplies. However, a separate officer was in command of the overall Confederate post of Camp Sumter. Each guard regiment had their own command staff of officers that outranked Wirz. The quartermaster's office operated independent of these two commands, as did the hospital. Wirz could request guards or rations, but had no direct authority to acquire these necessities, although he could order them withheld. Wirz's letters to his superiors in Richmond belie his desperation to solve this command debacle. In an effort to alleviate these bureaucratic struggles, General John Winder reported to Andersonville in the summer of 1864. However, he lacked a clear command directive, and the presence of a brigadier general further complicated the chain of command at the prison… Wirz was unable to control the bureaucracy that plagued the Confederate military prison system, so he controlled the prisoners in the only way he could – through intimidation and punishment."

Wirz was hated by the Union soldiers, and there are many accounts of his vile temper, profanity, hatred of Yankees, and his penchant for punishing "crimes" committed by the prisoners. These punishments included hunting prisoners with packs of wild dogs, shootings, chain gangs, being bucked or whipped, and being placed in the stockades. Wirz also prescribed balls and chains for many prisoners who broke his rules.

For his part, he usually delegated the most troublesome tasks, including executions, to the sentries and guards, and at his trial, he was charged with conspiracy "to impair and injure the health and destroy the lives of large numbers of federal prisoners." The charges against him included 11 counts of murder, and some former prisoners swore he himself had shot or otherwise killed men in his charge. In *The Tragedy of Andersonville: Trial of Captain Henry Wirz, the Prison Keeper*, author Norton Parker Chipman writes that a large number of Union soldiers, both black and white, testified to what Wirz had done, or the horrors of what his orders had brought about in terms of punishment. Martin E. Hogan, of the 1st Indiana Calvary, had this to say about his escape attempt: "I escaped from the prison about the 8th of October, and was captured about two days afterwards and brought back. After some of the most profane abuse from Captain Wirz that I ever heard from the lips of a man, I was ordered into the stocks. I was fastened at the neck and ankles and left to stay for sixty-eight hours without any food."[31]

Andrew J. Spring of the 16th Connecticut witnessed a multitude of chain gangs among the prisoners and described them: "I saw a chain-gang there; I have seen them every day; there were thirteen of them in it at one time. The men had to keep step with each other. Each man had a small ball (I do not know the weight of it) outside the leg, which he to carry in his hand when he traveled, and also a 64 pound ball to every four men. There was a large shackle around the neck with a large chain, much larger than that fastened to the legs around their necks, reaching around the circle."[32]

Spring also testified about one prisoner being shot for accidentally crossing the dead-line: "There was a man who was asleep under his blanket in the middle of the day. The stockade being so crowded, he had to lie near the dead-line. This man while he was asleep rolled over the dead-line. As soon as he rolled over he was shot."[33]

As bad as Andersonville was for everyone, black prisoners were often treated much worse, including frequently being whipped. Spring explained, "I have seen our darky prisoners hauled up and up there and receiving from fifty to seventy-five lashes a number of times."[34]

Jon F. Heath, a Rebel officer, testified that Wirz wouldn't hesitate to have savage dogs attack prisoners: "I saw a man in a tree, Captain Wirz ordered the man to come down. The man begged the dogs should not be let to hurt him. He made the man come down and with that the dogs rushed at him. Captain Wirz did not try to keep the dogs off the man; he could have done so."[35]

Joseph Keyser, of the 120th New York, had this to say about Wirz: "As a general thing I thought Captain Wirz was rather overbearing, and very profane and abusive in his language toward our men, on the slightest provocation. I never saw him buck any man - I have seen men bucked by his orders. I heard the orders given."[36]

James Mohan, a Rebel soldier, claimed, "I frequently hear Captain Wirz remark that he wished the prisoners were all in hell and he with them."

O.S. Belcher of the 16th Illinois Cavalry told a grisly anecdote about Wirz: "I heard Captain Wirz say he could kill more Yankees than they were killing at the front, I have seen twenty-thirty men killed at or around the dead-line and shot in different places around the stockade." [37]

James K Davidson of the 4th Iowa Calvary seconded the words of Belcher and mentioned other punishments: "I have heard Captain Wirz say he was killing more damned Yankees there than Lee was at Richmond. I have seen men who were starved to death, thousands of them, inside the stockade, I saw men eating food that they took from the ground; I have seen men pick up and eat undigested food that had passed through other men; I saw the chain-gang; I have seen from twelve to fourteen men in the chain-gang; they were kept out in the hot sun."[38]

Edwards S. Kellogg of the 20th New York Regiment was once bucked for six hours at Andersonville for failing to report a man who escaped. "They took a string and tied my wrists together in the first place; they sat me down on the ground next, put my hands over my knees and put a stick over my arms and under my legs, my hands being tied together."

Joseph R. Achuff was also punished harshly for trying to escape: "I tried to escape and was caught; I was put into the stocks in the broiling hot sun. For thirty-six hours I had nothing eat, but two drinks of water from that dirty creek. When I appealed to Captain Wirz, he told me to dry up, or he would blow my damned brains out, that I deserved to be hung. After I was [38]taken out of the stocks, I was ironed. I had shackles fastened around each leg, an iron ring, and a bar of iron between my legs. They kept my legs separated about eighteen inches, so that I had to shuffle along. There was nothing done to cure my legs. Scurvy fell into the wounds, but I was kept in irons….The water that ran through that stockade a horse would not drink. It was the filthiest stuff, with grease upon it. I complained to Captain Wirz and asked him if he could stop the grease from the cook house from being allowed to flow in there. He said it was good enough for me."[39]

Frank Maddox, a black soldier, discussed what the guards working under Wirz said about him: "The sergeant intimated to us that Captain Wirz gave the men a thirty days' furlough every time they shot a Yankee." Maddox also explained the punishment for a Union soldier who tried to blacken himself and escape: "When they wanted to punish them, they put them across a log and whipped them half to death and put them back to work..[it was] 'n*****'s law' if they tried to escape by blackening themselves." According to Maddox, the punishment was 39 lashes.[40]

Henry Jennings of the 8th United States Colored Troops relayed a story about the one day he was too injured to work, and the punishment he suffered because of it: "I was placed on duty about a month after I was put on the stockade. My wound was then bleeding. I was wounded through the thigh of the left leg. I received no medical attention.; they whipped me on my bare back. They made me bend over. …The whipping had no effect on my wound. Afterward they took me and put me in the stocks. I was kept there a day and a night. I did not get any food or drink while in the stocks."[41]

Another prisoner, Alexander Kennel, noted, "I have seen men who were balled and chained, and also men who were bucked and gagged by his [Wirz's] orders; I have seen them put into the stocks." [42]

John Fischer, a black soldier with the 8th U.S. Colored regiment, asserted, "I received very bad treatment there. I was bucked and gaggled, and whipped with thirty-nine lashes. I was bucked because I would not go back to work." [43]

Charles E. Smith, from company K of the 4th U.S. cavalry, saw four men shot at the stockade. One man "was reaching under the dead-line to pick up a piece of bread which some other man had thrown out of his haversack. The sentinel shot him from his post…the man died instantly. Captain Wirz was present."[44]

Robert Tatte, private of the 52nd Pennsylvania Volunteers, claimed he "saw Captain Wirz commit acts of cruelty..I saw him kick men who were not able to stand on their feet at roll-call, if there was trouble with roll call-no rations."[45]

Even Clara Barton relayed a story about a pregnant black worker and what she went through at

---

38 , 39, 40. Trial of Captain Henry Wirz, the Prison Keeper By Norton Parker Chipman

Andersonville. "The person is seated upon the ground, the knees drawn up, the hands put under the knees, and a stick run through over the arms and under the knees, the hands being tied in front; that makes them utterly immovable..then there is a gag put in the mouth and tied at the back of the head--this woman had been treated in that way--then the overseer had come behind her, kicked her on the back, and thrown her over. She had been stripped in the mean time, for they never whip the negro with the clothes on; she was thrown on her face, and lashed on her back, so that, when her husband found her, he said she was a gore of blood, and she must have been; she had been untied, and was lying there as she had been left."[46]

For all his cruelty, swagger, brandishing of pistols, and mistreatment of the prisoners at Andersonville, Wirz tried three times to improve the conditions of the prisoners. That said, his first decision, expanding the compound, was just common sense: "With prison badly overcrowded, its superintendent, Major Henry Wirz, authorized an expansion of the stockade. Using prisoner labor, a 610 ft. addition was built on the prison's north side. Built in two weeks, it was opened to the prisoners on July 1. Despite this 10-acre expansion, Andersonville remained badly overcrowded with the population peaking at 33,000 in August. Throughout the summer, conditions in the camp continued to deteriorate as the men, exposed to the elements, suffered from malnutrition and diseases such as dysentery."[47]

Wirz also tried a couple of times to facilitate prisoner exchanges: "By July 1864 Capt. Wirz actually paroled five Union prisoners to deliver a petition to Union officials. This note was signed by almost all of the Union prisoners. It asked for a reinstatement of the prisoner exchange program because the conditions at Andersonville were worse than deplorable. That petition was denied."[48]

In another attempt, the Confederates tried to deliver prisoners to the Union lines: "In a desperate attempt to relieve the situation at the prison, the Confederates carried thousands of prisoners by rail to Union lines at Jacksonville, Florida, and offered to turn them over to the Federal army. The prisoners were turned away by their own comrades and the South had no choice but to return them to Andersonville."[49]

In the end, Wirz was the only Confederate leader to be tried and executed for war crimes. Many Southerners insisted he did the best he could with a bad situation, a similar defense to the one they had for Winder (who died of a heart attack in February 1865), but the examples of his abusive behavior strongly suggest otherwise. The trial lasted for 63 days, involved 143 witnesses, and resulted in Wirz being found guilty and hanged.

This decision is still debated today, and a monument has been built in Andersonville, Georgia to pay homage to the convicted war criminal: "For nearly one hundred fifty years Henry Wirz has remained a polarizing figure. In 1866, President Andrew Johnson ordered a halt to further military tribunals, saving most of Wirz's named co-conspirators from suffering a similar fate. In the bitter years of Reconstruction, many Southerners turned to Wirz, the most prominent

Confederate to be punished for war crimes, as a symbolic martyr of their Lost Cause. Several former Confederates associated with the prison, including Surgeon Randolph Stevenson and Lt. Samuel Davis published books in defense of Wirz. Prisoners continued to publish memoirs vilifying the side of the man that they saw from inside the stockade – a cruel tyrant that threatened them and their comrades. In the heat of these acrimonious debates, conflicting mythologies emerged. Stories were fabricated – stories that Wirz had personally killed hundreds of men, or that the supposed star witness perjured himself, thus proving Wirz's innocence. Every story imaginable to absolve Wirz was concocted – placing blame on Generals Grant or Sherman, or even on the prisoners. A monument was erected in memory of Henry Wirz in the town of Andersonville that further reinforced these increasingly popular notions. In response, prisoners and their descendants further exaggerated the cruelties of Wirz. In the absence of scholarship on the man or the trial, these myths have permeated the popular understanding of Andersonville."[50]

Pictures of the death sentence being read to Wirz on the gallows shortly before the hanging

Picture of Wirz's execution moments after the trap door opened

Analysis of his conviction continues to this day in the south, but his war crimes are clear: "Whether or not Wirz violated the existing laws of war is not subject to debate. The existing legal frameworks of the day stipulated that prisoners must be given access to the same supplies available to the armies in the field. Wirz's own staff members, including his colleague from Richmond who also worked at Andersonville, George Gibbs, testified that Wirz failed to meet that legal obligation. His threats to kill or injure prisoners as a means of control by intimidation backfired on him and reinforced the belief that he was withholding things not to exact a degree of control, but to purposefully torment and kill his captives. The real debates and legacies of Henry Wirz are much bigger than his own actions in the prisons of Virginia, Alabama, and Georgia. Did the difficult circumstances of managing an overcrowded prison in a crumbling Confederacy justify Wirz's decisions and behavior? Should Wirz have been tried by a military tribunal or civil court? Was he legally protected from prosecution? What responsibilities do officers bear for their commands? These are difficult issues that have resurfaced again and again in our history. The legality and process of military justice continue to divide us well into the 21st century."[51]

Chapter 8: The Legacy of Andersonville

In the aftermath of the war, the Confederates cried foul that so much scorn was laid at the feet of Camp Sumter. The South largely claimed that their shrinking armies and lack of food and overcrowding accounted for Andersonville was such an atrocity, but the facts were more insidious.[61] To begin with, the Confederate treatment of black soldiers contributed to a breakdown of the exchanges, and the South's abusive treatment of the prisoners at Camp Sumter violated every norm and custom of warfare. "During the war, almost 45,000 prisoners were received at the Andersonville prison, and of these 12,913 died (40 percent of all the Union prisoners that died throughout the South). A continual controversy among historians is the nature of the deaths and the reasons for them. Some contend that it constituted deliberate Confederate war crimes toward Union prisoners; while others contend that it was merely the result of disease (promoted by severe overcrowding), the shortage of food in the Confederate States, the incompetence of the prison officials, and the refusal of the Confederate authorities to parole black soldiers, resulting in the imprisonment of soldiers from both sides, thus overfilling the stockade."[62]

Perhaps nobody could provide a better perspective than the prisoners themselves. John Maile witnessed the worst abuses of Andersonville but still tried to be fair when observing the big picture regarding the resources of the North and the South: For his part, he considered the Confederates at Andersonville to be criminally negligent:

> "In the movements of strategy and battle, many combatants were taken prisoners; these were sent to the rear for safe-keeping and maintenance. With practically unlimited resources this additional burden was scarcely felt at the North.
>
> At the South, the case was different. The extended territory occupied by the armies was practically unproductive for the people. It was, therefore, inevitable that the prisoners of war share the general limitation. As their numbers increased, it was necessary that they be conveyed to localities beyond the reach of rescue. Their increasing hosts could not wait upon the size of the stockades built for their confinement, and the limited forces that could be spared for their safe keeping must in some way hold them closely in hand.
>
> Moreover, unfriendly prejudices were increasing by the very fact of invasion, and as the North was held responsible for the war, the prisoners were the objects of bitter hatred. In numerous minor particulars, such as ample supply of water, of

62. Andersonville Prison. Retrieved at http://www.newworldencyclopedia.org/entry/Andersonville_prison

shelter and of food and fuel, the obligations of the southern military authorities were criminally negligent; yet many of the features of the prison circumstances were probably unavoidable...

One recollection has burned itself into memory. At Andersonville there was a standing offer of immediate release to any prisoner of average strength who would take the oath of allegiance to the Confederacy and engage in non-combatant service. Officers who entered the prison with these proposals were shunned by our men. I recall a recently naturalized Federal prisoner who thus enlisted. When he re-entered the prison in Confederate uniform as a recruiting officer, his reception was such that he fled to the gate for his life; shouting to the guard to protect him. For flag and country our boys could uncomplainingly die a lingering death, but they could not turn traitor."[63]

Monuments at Andersonville

Additional Online Resources

McElroy, John. Andersonville: A Story of Rebel Military Prisons Toledo: D.R. Locke, 1879.

Bibliography

Chipman, Norton P. The Horrors of Andersonville Rebel Prison. San Francisco: Bancroft, 1891.

Cloyd, Benjamin G. Haunted by Atrocity: Civil War Prisons in American Memory. (Louisiana State University Press, 2010)

Costa, Dora L; Kahn, Matthew E. "Surviving Andersonville: The Benefits of Social Networks in POW Camps," American Economic Review (2007) 97#4 pp. 1467–1487. econometrics

Futch, Ovid. "Prison Life at Andersonville," Civil War History (1962) 8#2 pp. 121–35 in Project MUSE

Futch, Ovid. History of Andersonville Prison (1968)

Genoways, Ted & Hugh H. Genoways (eds.). A Perfect Picture of Hell: Eyewitness Accounts by Civil War Prisoners from the 12th Iowa. Iowa City: University of Iowa Press, 2001.

Marvel, William. Andersonville: The Last Depot (University of North Carolina Press, 1994) excerpt and text search

Pickenpaugh, Roger. Captives in Blue: The Civil War Prisons of the Confederacy (2013) pp. 119–66

Ransom, John. Andersonville Diary. Auburn, NY: Author, 1881.

Rhodes, James, History of the United States from the Compromise of 1850, vol. V. New York: Macmillan, 1904.

Spencer, Ambrose, A Narrative of Andersonville. New York: Harper, 1866.

Stevenson, R. Randolph. The Southern Side, or Andersonville Prison. Baltimore: Turnbull, 1876.

Voorhees, Alfred H. The Andersonville Prison Diary of Alfred H. Voorhees. 1864.

Made in the USA
Middletown, DE
03 December 2016